Property Disputes in Indian Families

Historical, Psychological and Legal Aspects

By Siva Prasad Bose and Joy Bose

Published by Joy Bose

Copyright 2022 Joy Bose

All Rights Reserved

Contents

Preface

Chapter 1: History of Family Property Disputes in India

Chapter 2: Psychology of Sibling Rivalries and Psychological Impact of Property Disputes

Chapter 3: Statistics of Property Related Court Cases in India

Chapter 4: Law Related to Succession of Property in India

Chapter 5: Law Related to Transfer of Property in India

Chapter 6: Procedure for Fighting Property Court Cases

Chapter 7: The Role of Women in Property Disputes

Chapter 8: Property Disputes in NRIs and Overseas Indians

Chapter 9: Alternative Dispute Resolution (ADR) for Property Disputes

Chapter 10: Conclusion

About the Authors

Glossary of Key Legal Terms

Books by Siva Prasad Bose

Preface

Property and land disputes take up the largest proportion of cases in Indian courts. A significant number of such disputes are within families, with siblings and cousins fighting with each other. This creates an unnecessary drain on the economy and on productivity. They are also among the most emotionally and financially draining conflicts that families in India face. Whether it is a fight over ancestral land, inheritance battles between siblings, or legal tussles over property transfers, such disputes have become a defining feature of Indian society. They not only consume time and resources but also create deep, often irreparable, rifts within families.

This book seeks to explore the multi-faceted nature of family property disputes in India. It delves into their historical roots, psychological underpinnings, legal complexities, and possible solutions. Through a comprehensive analysis, we attempt to answer key questions: Why do families fight over property? What are the legal avenues available for resolving such conflicts? How can individuals safeguard their assets while maintaining family harmony?

Our journey begins with a historical perspective, tracing property disputes back to ancient India. From the legendary conflicts in the Mahabharata and Ramayana to the dynastic struggles of Mughal and Maratha rulers, history is rife with examples of families torn apart over land and inheritance. These stories provide crucial insights into the nature of property disputes and highlight that these conflicts are not merely about material wealth but are often driven by deeper psychological and social factors.

In subsequent chapters, we explore the psychology behind sibling rivalries, entitlement, and the long-term impact of property disputes on mental well-being. Family dynamics, favoritism, and perceived injustices often lay the foundation for bitter legal battles later in life. By understanding these psychological factors, families can take proactive steps to prevent conflicts before they escalate into full-blown disputes.

The legal landscape of property ownership, inheritance, and transfer in India is vast and intricate. We provide a clear, reader-friendly overview of the key laws governing succession, transfer of property, and inheritance rights. Whether you are dealing with ancestral property, drafting a will, or caught in a legal battle, this book serves as a guide to navigating India's complex property laws.

A significant portion of property disputes end up in the overburdened Indian courts, where cases can drag on for decades. We discuss legal strategies, court procedures, and the pros and cons of different dispute resolution mechanisms. For those seeking alternatives to litigation, we also examine the growing importance of mediation and arbitration as effective means of settling property conflicts.

Women's rights in property inheritance have been historically neglected, but recent legal changes have brought about significant improvements. We explore the evolving legal status of women's property rights, landmark court rulings, and the persistent challenges women face in claiming their rightful inheritance.

Property disputes are particularly challenging for Non-Resident Indians (NRIs) and overseas Indians who own assets in India but struggle to manage or protect them from fraudulent claims and encroachments. We address the unique challenges faced by NRIs, legal remedies available, and preventive measures that can be taken to safeguard property from illegal occupation.

This book is not just about legal battles; it is about understanding and addressing the deeper issues that lead to them. Through knowledge, planning, and open communication, families can prevent property disputes and preserve relationships while securing their assets.

We hope that this book serves as a valuable resource for anyone navigating the complexities of property inheritance and ownership in India. By learning from history, understanding psychology, and leveraging legal tools, we can move towards a future where property remains a source of security rather than conflict.

Chapter 1: History of Family Property Disputes in India

In this chapter we trace the history of property disputes within Indian families, from ancient mythology to the modern era. Understanding this long arc of conflict helps us appreciate why such disputes are so deeply embedded in Indian society, and why they so often tear families apart.

India is no stranger to property and land disputes. We have plenty of tales from mythology and history to show that within the family in the absence of a strong heir or a clearly defined successor to the land. Usually, after the death of a patriarch, the brothers fought each other for the right to the land. However, disputes within a family are not limited to brothers and can also include other members such as uncles, or even between a father and son for control of the kingdom.

1.1 Family property disputes in Indian mythology

The ancient Indian epics Ramayana and Mahabharata speak of property disputes within joint families.

In Ramayana, king Dasharatha of Ayodhya had four sons and was planning to give the kingdom to the eldest son Rama, but the mother of a younger brother Bharata wanted her son to gain the kingdom, so she persuaded the king to banish Rama to the forest so that her son could rule the kingdom.

In Mahabharata, two groups of cousin brothers, Pandavas and Kauravas, fought a war with each other for the right to rule the kingdom. The Pandava brothers eventually won the war, but at a great human cost and all the Kaurava brothers died in the war.

A similar rivalry is described among the king Bharata Chakravartin of Ayodhya and his brother Bahubali, sons of the Jain king Rishabhanath.

1.2 Family property disputes in ancient India

The fight between king Bimbisara and his son Ajatshatru of the Magadha kingdom in 5th century BC is well known. Ajatshatru imprisoned his father Bimbisara and later had him killed, and thus snatched the kingdom.

There were similar fights of succession between emperor Ashoka and his brothers in the Mauryan kingdom. The Buddhist Pali texts Mahavamsa and Dipavamsa state that Ashoka killed several of his brothers before ascending the throne.

1.3 Family property disputes in the Rashtrakuta kingdom

The Rashtrakuta kingdom of the 8th century AD had disputes between brothers Govinda II and Dhruva Dharavarsha. Eventually, Dhruva defeated his unpopular brother and ascended the throne.

Similarly, the later Rashtrakuta kingdom of 10th century AD had a dispute between brothers Amoghavarsha II and Govinda IV who assassinated his brother and grabbed the throne.

1.4 Property disputes between Prithviraj and Jaichand kingdoms

In the 12th century AD, King Jaichand of Gahadwala dynasty and King Prithviraj Chauhan of Delhi were supposedly cousins and their rivalry is made famous by the legend of Prithviraj Raso, although its authenticity is somewhat debatable.

1.5 Family property disputes in the Pandyan kingdom

The Pandyan kingdom of south India in 14th century AD had a rivalry between brothers Vira Pandya and Sundara Pandya. As it happened, Sundara Pandya invited the Khalji rulers of Delhi to invade his brother Vira Pandya's kingdom, leading to the loss of its independence.

1.6 Family property disputes in the Vijayanagar empire

The Vijaynagara empire of South India had its own share of family rivalries after the death of the powerful ruler Krishna Deva Raya in 16th century AD.

A notable rivalry was between Aliya Rama Raya and Sadashiva Raya. Sadashiva Raya was appointed king when still a minor, but was dethroned and kept a prisoner by Aliya Rama Raya.

1.7 Family property disputes in Mughal empire

In the medieval era, India again has seen plenty of property disputes between siblings, mainly in royal houses but also among ordinary landowning people. Usually when the patriarch, such as the Mughal emperor dies, his sons start squabbling among themselves for the right to win the kingdom and this leads to a lot of bloodshed.

Mughal emperors who had sibling rivalries included emperor Humayun, who had to fight for the kingdom with his brothers Kamran, Askari and Hindal.

Emperor Shah Jahan had a similar fight with his half-brother prince Khusrou and other brothers, before he could win the Mughal throne.

The most famous rivalry was with the sons of Shah Jahan. As the emperor Shah Jahan became old, he appointed one of his sons, Dara Shikoh, as the heir to the kingdom. But the other sons were not happy with this and raised armies and started fighting. Ultimately, the youngest son, Aurangzeb, won the throne and killed his brothers and even imprisoned his own father Shah Jahan.

1.8 Family property disputes in the Maratha empire

The Maratha empire had a similar rivalry between Shivaji's sons Shambhaji and his younger half-brother Rajaram in the 17th century AD. Rajaram was installed as king at the age of ten by his step-mother who plotted with the nobles against Shambhaji. But soon Shambhaji fought back and jailed his brother and the other conspirators.

The Peshwa rulers of Pune also had their own family rivalries and tensions.

1.9 Family property disputes in the Rajput kingdoms

Other sibling rivalries in the medieval era included the Rajput kings as well. This included the rivalry between Sawai Jai Singh of Amber and his younger brother Bijay Singh in 18th century AD after the death of Aurangzeb, during the Rajput rebellion of 1708 against the Mughal empire.

1.10 Family property disputes in the Bengal kingdom

Mir Jafar and his son in law Mir Qasim, nawabs of Bengal also had a family rivalry during the 18th century AD. Mir Qasim was made the nawab of Bengal by the East India Company replacing his father-in-law Mir Jafar.

Later, when Mir Qasim proved troublesome and fought the battle of Buxar with the British, the British defeated him and again installed Mir Jafar as the nawab.

1.11 Family property disputes in the British era

After the British came to India and established their rule over the whole of India, wars between kings became much less, but property disputes between siblings continued as always. This too was at all levels and all strata of society including between Zamindars and small farmers and princely states and industrialists. British established courts such as the high court of Calcutta had to deal with a number of property disputes.

1.12 Family property disputes in independent India

After independence, India has also seen a number of property disputes within joint families. India's wealthiest and most powerful families have fought bitterly over land, inheritance, and business assets. These high-profile cases have been played out in courts, boardrooms, and sometimes even in the media, serving as cautionary tales about the perils of unresolved family conflicts over property. A few of the ones involving famous people such as politicians and industrialists are well known.

The Ambani Brothers – A Billionaire Feud

No property battle in India has been as publicized as the feud between Mukesh Ambani and Anil Ambani, the sons of legendary business tycoon Dhirubhai Ambani. After their father's untimely death in 2002, without a will, the future of the massive Reliance conglomerate was thrown into chaos.

What Happened?

- The brothers could not agree on the division of assets, with Mukesh wanting to control everything and Anil demanding his rightful share.
- Their mother, Kokilaben Ambani, intervened and brokered a deal in 2005, dividing the business empire between the two.
- Mukesh took over Reliance Industries (oil, gas, telecom), while Anil got Reliance Communications, Infrastructure, and Power.

The Fallout

- Mukesh thrived, expanding Reliance into a trillion-dollar empire.
- Anil's businesses struggled, and he eventually declared bankruptcy in 2020.
- The feud continued as Mukesh's Jio took over the telecom industry, effectively eliminating Anil's Reliance Communications.

Lesson Learned: Families should ensure clear succession planning to avoid conflicts that can destroy business empires.

The Hinduja Brothers – A War Over Family Wealth

The Hinduja Group, a multi-billion-dollar business empire, has been controlled by four billionaire brothers—Srichand, Gopichand,

Prakash, and Ashok. But in 2020, a shocking legal battle broke out among them.

What Happened?

- The dispute revolved around a 2014 letter signed by all four brothers, stating that "everything belongs to everyone and nothing belongs to anyone."
- Srichand, the eldest brother, later claimed that this agreement should not apply to his assets, leading to a legal dispute with the other three brothers.
- The case went to court in the UK, highlighting deep fractures within the family.

The Fallout

- Srichand's health deteriorated, and the case added immense stress to the family.
- The brothers tried to settle the case outside court, but the damage to their relations was already done.

Lesson Learned: When dealing with shared business wealth, a written legal agreement defining each member's stake is crucial.

The Singhania Family and the Raymond Group Dispute

The famous Raymond brand, known for its premium suiting fabrics, became the centre of an ugly legal dispute between father Vijaypat Singhania and son Gautam Singhania.

What Happened?

- Vijaypat handed over the family business, Raymond, to his son Gautam in 2015.

- He later claimed that Gautam had turned against him, denied him access to his own wealth, and refused to provide him with a place to live.
- The case turned into a dramatic public spectacle, with Vijaypat giving interviews accusing his son of betrayal.

The Fallout

- A legal battle ensued, tarnishing the reputation of the Singhania family.
- The feud exposed how gifting family wealth without legal safeguards can lead to bitter disputes.

Lesson Learned: Parents should not blindly transfer assets to their children without securing their financial future.

The Birla Estate Feud – A Mystery Will

One of the most complex property battles in India was the Birla family dispute, triggered by an alleged 'mystery will'.

What Happened?

- Priyamvada Birla, widow of M.P. Birla, left behind an enormous estate worth thousands of crores.
- A will surfaced claiming that she left the entire fortune to her accountant, R.S. Lodha, instead of the Birla family.
- The Birlas challenged the will, alleging fraud and foul play.

The Fallout

- A decades-long court battle ensued.

- The case raised serious questions about will authenticity and the role of trusted advisors in family wealth disputes.

Lesson Learned: Every family should keep wills properly documented, legally registered, and ensure multiple trustworthy witnesses.

The Bajaj Family Rift Over Wealth Distribution

The Bajaj Group, a powerful conglomerate in India, faced an internal battle over inheritance.

What Happened?

- Rahul Bajaj, the head of the Bajaj empire, was reportedly at odds with his cousins over how the business should be run.
- The disagreement led to splits within the family.
- Eventually, the business was divided into different companies to resolve conflicts.

The Fallout

- Though the split was amicable compared to other cases, the divisions changed the landscape of the Bajaj business empire.

Lesson Learned: Pre-planned business divisions can prevent bitter disputes and ensure smooth transitions.

These high-profile cases provide some crucial lessons for all families, whether rich or middle-class:

- **Make a Clear Will** – Never leave inheritance decisions ambiguous. Legal wills prevent confusion and conflict.

- **Avoid Favoritism** – Parents should ensure fair distribution to prevent jealousy among siblings.
- **Involve a Neutral Legal Mediator** – Independent mediators can help settle disputes before they escalate to courts.
- **Discuss Inheritance Openly** – Families should have open discussions about wealth distribution to avoid surprises and resentments later.
- **Don't Rely on Verbal Promises** – All agreements must be legally documented to prevent future legal battles.

Even India's most powerful families have crumbled due to poorly managed property disputes. By learning from these cases, families can avoid similar pitfalls and ensure that property and wealth do not turn loved ones into bitter enemies.

1.13 Conclusion

The historical account of property disputes in India reveals that conflicts over inheritance and land are deeply rooted in our culture and society. From ancient royal feuds to modern-day legal battles, the underlying causes remain largely the same—power struggles, familial rivalries, and unclear succession planning. Understanding these historical patterns helps us recognize the long-standing nature of property conflicts and underscores the importance of legal and social frameworks to address them effectively. In the next chapter, we explore the psychological dimensions of property disputes, delving into how sibling rivalries and familial dynamics contribute to these conflicts.

References

- Majumdar, R. C. (1951). The history and culture of the Indian people.
- Wikipedia. Jatavarman Vira Pandyan II https://en.wikipedia.org/wiki/Jatavarman_Vira_Pandyan_II
- Wikipedia. Bahubali. https://en.wikipedia.org/wiki/Bahubali
- Wikipedia. Ashoka. https://en.wikipedia.org/wiki/Ashoka
- Wikipedia. Ajatshatru. https://en.wikipedia.org/wiki/Ajatashatru
- Wikipedia. Dhruva Dharavarsha. https://en.wikipedia.org/wiki/Dhruva_Dharavarsha
- Wikipedia. Rajput Rebellion 1708-1710. https://en.wikipedia.org/wiki/Rajput_Rebellion_1708-1710
- Suman Layak. In the name of the mother. Business Today, Nov 2009. https://www.businesstoday.in/magazine/cover-story/story/in-the-name-of-the-mother-244519-2009-11-13
- The Economic Times. June 2020. Hinduja Vs Hinduja; Ambani Brothers In Arms, And Other Family Feuds Of India Inc. https://economictimes.indiatimes.com/magazines/panache/singh-vs-singh-and-other-family-feuds-that-shook-up-india-inc/ets-dualpane-12/slideshow/65682537.cms
- SCMP, 5 August 2021. Will the Singhania family feud ever end? Billionaire Gautam and father Vijaypat have been locked in legal battles over Raymond Group and their luxury real estate since 2015. https://www.scmp.com/magazines/style/celebrity/article/3143797/will-singhania-family-feud-ever-end-billionaire-gautam

Key Takeaways — Chapter 1

Property disputes within Indian families have existed since ancient times, as shown by the Ramayana and Mahabharata. Royal dynasties from the Mauryas to the Mughals repeatedly suffered succession crises caused by unclear inheritance rules. Modern industrialist families — the Ambanis, Hindujas, Singhanias, and Birlas — show that wealth alone does not prevent bitter disputes. The single most effective preventive measure, across all eras, is clear and legally documented succession planning. Verbal promises and informal understandings invariably become the source of conflict; written legal agreements are essential.

Chapter 2: Psychology of Sibling Rivalries and Psychological Impact of Property Disputes

In this chapter we discuss the psychology behind family rivalries, in particular the most common form which is the rivalry between siblings. We also discuss the psychological impact of property disputes. Most of the theories hold that experiences early in life can cause rivalries in siblings, and further psychological problems when the siblings grow up to be adults. If the experiences are largely positive, the children may grow into healthy adults. But if the reverse is true, problems can happen.

Brothers and sisters often grow up competing for their parents' attention, which can shape sibling relationships later in life. The parents may show favoritism to one sibling, which can foster resentment and lead to property disputes later in life.

On top of it, siblings keep on getting compared to each other, especially in terms of achievements, by the rest of society. This creates a sense of rivalry and jealousy, which may manifest later in life in things such as property disputes. There might also be feelings of entitlement and victimization by one or more siblings, feelings that they are entitled to their share and have been unjustly treated by their parents and so on.

We first discuss a few psychology theories related to developmental and family psychology. Our aim is to understand how sibling rivalries develop over time.

2.1 Freud's theory of development

As per the psychosocial theory of development by Sigmund Freud and other psychologists, many or most of our problems stem from our childhood. Our mind has three aspects: the conscious mind that we are aware of, the subconscious and the unconscious mind which has latent or hidden impulses. Accordingly, the experiences we have had as children shape our view of the world.

As per **Freud's Psychoanalytical Model** of development, the infant goes through different psychosexual stages in early development such as oral, anal, phallic, latency etc. If during any of these stages the development is not ideal, this can lead to psychological issues later in life.

Also, there is a constant interplay between three factors in the mind: id, ego and superego.

- Id is driven by basic and primal instinctual needs such as pleasure and hunger, not considering the needs of others. This is predominant in babies, who cry when their needs are not being fulfilled.
- Ego is more balanced, considers the reality of each situation and balances our own needs with those of others in the world.
- Superego is the voice of our conscience and morality and typically also develops later in life.

So in cases where the ego, id and superego are not balanced from an early age, a person may grow to have issues later in life, including issues with their siblings.

2.2 Melanie Klein's Object Relations Theory

Melanie Klein was a developmental psychologist who came after Freud. She developed a theory of relationships called **Object**

Relations Theory, such as the relation between a mother and a child.

As per the theory, the child projects good and bad, love and hate feelings upon separate parts of its mother, depending on whether their needs are being met and to what extent.

David Winnicott, another developmental psychologist, further developed Klein's theory and suggested that psychological difficulties develop during the baby's growth if the environment, including the mother, fail to satisfy their needs on a regular and reliable basis.

2.3 John Bowlby's Attachment Theory

As per the **Theory of Attachment** postulated by the developmental psychologist John Bowlby, the relationship of the child with their mother is essential to how they develop later in life. The quality and nature of the bond with the mother, and how the child is cared for in their early years, is crucial in forming the child's world view.

If the child's initial experiences are positive and they have the feeling of being loved, they will develop a healthy and secure view of the world. On the other hand, if their initial experiences are of being unloved, their view of the world will be similar.

2.4 Systemic Therapy and Structural Family Therapy

A number of psychologists in the 1960s, especially in the Palo Alto Mental Research Institute, postulated the idea of **Systemic Therapy**. Their main idea was that communication of members within the family and other social circles is most important. Later problems in one's individual psychology can be traced to one's social relationships, such as within the family and one's social circle. The language used in communication within the family define the values and relationships.

For example, lots of friction and quarreling between the adults in the family, such as one's parents, may cause the children to themselves become disruptive at school or later in life. Hence, by understanding this and altering the interactions between family members to more healthy interactions, we can create conditions for a healthier development of the children within the family.

The theory of **Structural Family Therapy** emerged from these. This states that dynamics, power relations and boundaries within the family shape the individuals' psychological development. How the parents enforce the rules and boundaries for their kids, how the rules and family hierarchy is structured, how the family copes with difficult external situations, are all important factors.

For example, a child can learn in a family that the more they are disruptive, the more attention they get from their parents. This may end up in their developing into narcissist and psychopathic individuals when they grow up, not caring for the feelings of others and doing whatever it takes to meet their aims in their corporate career or in terms of getting hold of property within the family.

The later Milan School of psychologists further developed the theories of family therapy. They postulated that the values and communication within the family are very important. Meaning is created through the family values and communication, and it is a dynamic and changing process.

2.5 Psychology of sibling rivalries in India

From the above theories, we can understand that a lot of the roots of the sibling rivalries, which later manifest into property disputes, may emerge from an early age, from relationships and dynamics within the family, especially the relationships of the siblings with their parents.

In the families where the parents make an effort to consciously maintain a healthy relationship between siblings, such rivalries are less likely to happen. But if the family does not have established mechanisms for resolving problems and disputes within family members, this might lead to issues.

Unfortunately, in places like India, where there are limited resources and too much competition, such healthy trends are less likely to occur in families. Children in the family, especially brothers, are constantly compared to each other and even compared with the achievements of their parents, not only by their parents but also by other relatives and wider society. This creates an unhealthy environment where there is too much expectation and pressure on the kids.

Added to this can be the problem of favoritism by parents to one sibling compared to another. The resultant rivalry and jealousy a kid may have towards their own brothers and sisters when growing up may result into bad relations and disputes later on.

2.6 Research papers about understanding of property rights among young siblings

A journal paper by the psychologist H. S. Ross (1996) theorized the presence of entitlement and negotiations in arguments among siblings from early childhood, which was a possible cause of sibling rivalries turning into property disputes at a later age.

They studied a sample of interactions between siblings who were children and their parents, focusing on the language used that showed a sense of entitlement. They found that usually the parents would be able to intervene and resolve disagreements and arguments about possession and ownership of belongings, such as toys, among the siblings. However, the parents did not clearly distinguish between possession and ownership. At a later age, the parents may not be there to mediate the disputes and prevent them.

Other studies by Rossano et. al (2011) and Blake and Harris (2009) focused on the understanding of ownership and property rights among young children, manifested in the language used when speaking of their belongings.

From the above theories we can conclude that the root of most sibling property disputes may lie in the experiences developed during childhood and while growing up.

Feelings of entitlement, phenomena such as jealousy, sense of favoritism by parents, lack of care during childhood, all may contribute to the resentment built up, which may manifest in siblings squabbling over property in the courts.

2.7 Psychological impact of property disputes

Property disputes are not just legal battles; they are deeply personal conflicts that can tear families apart, cause immense stress, and even lead to depression and anxiety. Whether the dispute is over ancestral property, a will, or illegal occupation, the emotional toll is often severe. A prolonged legal battle over property can lead to:

- **Chronic Stress:** Worrying about case outcomes, legal fees, and court delays.
- **Anxiety and Depression:** Emotional breakdowns due to family conflicts and financial losses.
- **Sleep Disorders:** Insomnia caused by excessive worry and uncertainty.

- **Broken Family Bonds:** Permanent damage to relationships with parents, siblings, or relatives.
- **Social Embarrassment:** Public legal battles can lead to social stigma and gossip.

The Emotional Cost of Family Property Disputes manifests in multiple ways:

Parent-Child Conflicts

- In some cases, aging parents are pressured to transfer property to specific children.
- Siblings accuse each other of **manipulating** elderly parents.
- **Case Study:** An 80-year-old father was dragged to court by his son over property distribution. The stress led to severe health deterioration.

Sibling Rivalries and Betrayal

- Property disputes often worsen **childhood rivalries**.
- One sibling may feel they are being unfairly treated, leading to permanent estrangement.
- **Case Study:** Two sisters fought over their mother's house. The case lasted 15 years, and by the time it was settled, they had stopped speaking forever.

Spouse and In-Laws Pressure

- Sometimes, a person is pressured by their spouse or in-laws to claim a larger share in family property.
- This can lead to **marital stress** and even **divorce**.

2.8 Managing the Stress of Property Disputes

Property disputes may not be resolved overnight, but managing stress effectively can help you stay emotionally stable.

Focus on What You Can Control

- You cannot control court delays, but you **can** manage your reactions.
- Stay **organized** by keeping all legal documents in order.
- Seek legal advice early to avoid unnecessary anxiety.

Avoid Constantly Thinking About the Case

- Obsessing over the dispute can lead to anxiety and poor mental health.
- Set aside **dedicated time** to deal with legal matters but don't let them consume your entire life.

Seek Professional Support

- Consider talking to a **therapist or counselor**.
- Meditation and yoga can help **reduce stress and anxiety**.
- **Example:** A businessman fighting a lengthy land dispute practiced mindfulness to manage his frustration and anger.

Explore Alternative Resolutions

- Consider **mediation or arbitration** to avoid prolonged litigation.
- Many families have successfully resolved disputes through **family discussions** with neutral mediators.

Maintain Financial Stability

- Long legal battles can drain finances. Plan your budget wisely.
- **Tip:** Set aside a legal fund to manage unexpected legal expenses without financial stress.

2.9 Conclusion

Psychological factors, particularly sibling rivalries, favouritism, and feelings of entitlement, play a crucial role in property disputes. As we have seen, childhood experiences and family dynamics shape adult conflicts, leading to emotionally charged legal battles over inheritance and property ownership. The stress and trauma associated with such disputes can have lasting effects on mental health and family relationships. Moving forward, we will examine the statistical landscape of property-related court cases in India to understand the scale of these disputes and their impact on the judicial system.

References:

- Blake, P. R., & Harris, P. L. (2009). Children's understanding of ownership transfers. Cognitive Development, 24(2), 133-145.
- Bretherton, I. (1992). The origins of attachment theory: John Bowlby and Mary Ainsworth. Developmental psychology, 28(5), 759.
- Dallos, R., & Draper, R. (2015). An Introduction to Family Therapy: Systemic Theory and Practice. McGraw-Hill Education (UK).
- Jacobs, M. (1995). DW Winnicott. Sage.

- Milivojeviæ, L., & Iveziæ, S. (2004). Importance of object relations theories for development of capacity for mature love. J Croat Med, 45, 18-23.
- Milton, J., Polmear, C., & Fabricius, J. (2011). A short introduction to psychoanalysis. Sage.
- Rossano, F., Rakoczy, H., & Tomasello, M. (2011). Young children's understanding of violations of property rights. Cognition, 121(2), 219-227.
- Ross, H. S. (1996). Negotiating principles of entitlement in sibling property disputes. Developmental Psychology, 32(1), 90.

Key Takeaways — Chapter 2

Sibling rivalries that later manifest as property disputes often have roots in childhood experiences. Parental favouritism, constant comparisons, and unresolved feelings of entitlement create resentments that may surface decades later in legal battles. Psychological theories from Freud, Bowlby, and systems therapists all point to family dynamics as the foundation. Property disputes carry a heavy psychological toll, including chronic stress, anxiety, depression, and permanently damaged family bonds. Seeking professional counselling and considering mediation can help reduce the emotional burden of a protracted dispute.

Chapter 3: Statistics of Property Related Court Cases in India

Property dispute and land dispute related court cases are the longest pending and the highest number (about 66%) clogging the Indian court system. A significant number of these property disputes are likely to be within the same family, however the exact numbers are not known.

In this chapter we focus on the scale of property disputes in Indian courts, in terms of numbers of such court cases and time taken to resolve the cases.

Property and land disputes are bad for all parties involved. They lead to high litigation costs with no productive results, and are a burden on the economy. Sometimes the property disputes take decades or even generations to resolve. Often, they are related to inheritance and succession within the same family, in which case they further lead to bad blood within the family. Such disputes affect all classes of people: even the richest families of industrialists are not immune to them.

3.1 Data on the scale of property disputes in India

A 2016 newspaper article, based on a study by Daksh, mentioned that land and property cases account for two thirds of all pending civil court cases in India, including 7.5 million civil cases. Total cost of such litigation was 0.5% of India's GDP.

Another report by Center for policy research (CPR) found the following:

- Property disputes affect around 7.7 million people in India.

- Property disputes clog every level of courts in India from district and lower courts to supreme court.
- Property disputes are the largest both in terms of absolute numbers and time taken to resolve the cases.
- About 25% of all cases decided by the Supreme Court involve property disputes.
- Property disputes make up 66% of all civil cases in India.
- The average time taken to resolve a property dispute, from creation of the dispute to resolution by the Supreme Court, is 20 years.

An article in the Wire magazine analyzed government data to find that 37 lakhs cases in Indian courts took 0–20 years to reach a verdict, 6.4 lakh cases took 20–30 years and about 2 lakh cases took more than 30 years.

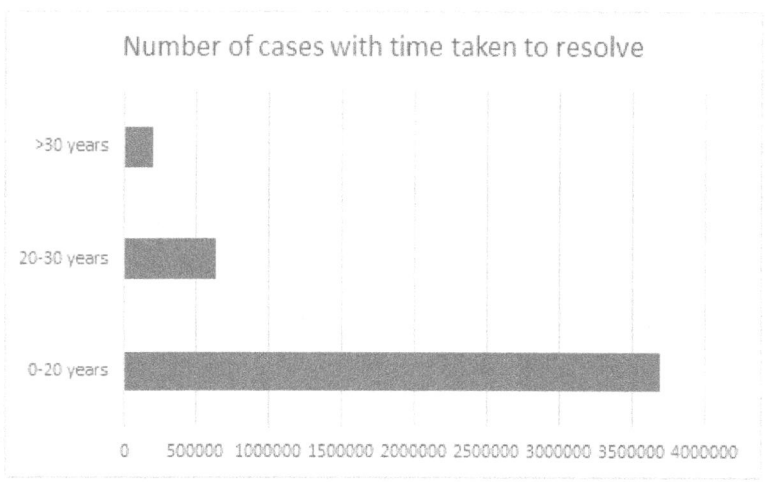

Figure: Graph showing the number of cases, with time taken to resolve them (in years)

India has almost 4 crore total pending cases in Supreme court, high courts and lower courts, as of 2020. This is as per a written reply by the government in parliament, published in a Bloomberg quint article. Of these 70% are civil cases and remaining 30% are criminal cases. In the high courts and supreme courts, most of the pending cases are civil cases, while the criminal cases are more in lower courts. This number has further increased since then because of the Covid-19 lockdowns, and is close to 4.5 crore.

3.2 Types of property cases in Indian courts

Property and land disputes encompass a wide variety of cases in Indian courts.

In this section we look at a few types of property cases.

3.2.1 Property cases related to succession

Cases related to succession and inheritance (especially concerning the Hindu Succession Act 1925) encompass a good percentage of the pending property cases in Indian courts. These can encompass cases related to probating the will of the person, or division of the property among legal heirs in absence of a will and so on.

Usually, such cases start when the patriarch or matriarch of a joint family dies and the siblings or other relatives fight each other to gain a larger share of the property left by the deceased person.

3.2.2 Property cases related to registration of land records

Some of the property cases occur when a buyer buys some property and finds out it is not registered properly with the land authorities or municipal authorities by the previous owners. It is then a painstaking process to prove that they are the owners and get the property registered in their names.

There are rules related to which land is allocated for agriculture, which for residential areas and which for industry, and rules on how to petition for conversion of land use. If such rules are violated, then again proving the legality of the property is a difficult process.

Registering a property in many states of India is a difficult process, involving things like giving bribes to the municipal authorities.

Sometimes the builders of an apartment complex or villa may have not done the construction of part of the flats in an authorized manner as per the rules of the municipality. There are a number of complex rules related to how much boundary to keep, what is the size of balcony and common areas, how much parking space is allocated and so on, which may be broken during construction and can lead to problems in getting the property legalized.

3.2.3 Property cases due to fraud and other crimes

Some of the ongoing property cases may be related to fraudulent transactions, such as when a person has been fraudulently deprived of their rightful claim on the land or property. There can also be other crimes involved, such as forcing a person to give up their property rights using threats and intimidation.

3.2.4 Property cases due to tenancy

Some of the cases may be due to a tenant refusing to vacate their land when their tenancy period has expired. The landlord would be forced to fight a case for many years to get back the possession of their own property, while the tenant continued to enjoy their stay.

3.2.5 Property cases due to trespassing or illegal occupation

Some of the property cases may be related to trespassing or illegal occupation of part or whole of the property. It could be by a relative or a neighbor or even a stranger. This can be the case where the original owner has been away for a while and the opposite party has encroached on their property or made unauthorized construction on the property. This is a common problem in case of Non Resident Indians (NRIs), who might be away for some years and working in a foreign country and unable to monitor their property closely.

In property cases, the rule seems to be that "possession is king". Whoever has already got possession of the property, whether by legal means or by hook or crook, it is an uphill task to dislodge them by the courts.

On top of this, rules such as "adverse possession" after 12 years give an incentive for people to knowingly trespass on someone else's land for hope of getting it after 12 years.

3.3 Reasons for the huge number of property disputes

There are multiple reasons for the huge number of pending property cases in Indian courts. One problem is lots of exceptions in the law and the complexities of the cases. There are a number of laws related to inheritance, such as Indian Succession act, 1925. There are different variances in the succession laws for Muslims and Christians and Hindus.

There are also a number of exceptions and special clauses in various laws, for example in states like Uttaranchal, Himachal Pradesh and North East, where only people who are domiciled are allowed to own land.

This creates a situation where there are too many laws and a common man has no choice but to take the help of expensive lawyers and court cases to enforce their property rights using the applicable laws.

3.4 Suggestions to lower the number of pending property cases

In this section, we discuss a few ways in which the number of pending property related cases can be reduced. Some of the ways to reduce the number and time of resolution of property cases are as follows:

- Courts can upgrade the infrastructure to have more virtual hearings rather than physical hearings. These can be facilitated by widely available online meeting software such as Zoom, Google meet, Microsoft teams or Cisco Webex. This will reduce the need for unnecessary travel by the litigants.
- The Government can amend and simplify the property related laws. This would clarify confusion and thus reduce the need for pending cases. They can reduce the number of exceptions and special cases in property related laws and try to make the laws uniform across India.
- Courts can better facilitate the opposite parties to mediate and resolve the disputes themselves. Although such mechanisms with court appointed mediators currently exist, they may not always be effective in reaching an agreement.
- Courts can further encourage mechanisms like lok adalats to more efficiently resolve property related disputes, and thus reduce the burden on regular courts.
- High courts and supreme court can publish a few guidelines and best practices that might facilitate the speedy resolutions of property disputes.

- The courts can define some maximum length of time within which a judgment must be made in property related cases
- Courts can prioritize long pending property disputes.
- The government can act to reduce corruption in government bodies such as city municipalities, land registration offices and the police. This alone can reduce the number of pending property cases.
- Courts can introduce some ways to make judges accountable. Or else, they can experiment with alternative kinds of judgment such as a jury system, which is common in some countries like USA.
- Courts can institute processes to give speedier interim relief in some kinds of property disputes, such as trespass related cases.
- The government can help with the digitalization of land records and regularization of property records such as A-katha and B-katha in Karnataka state. This would make it easier to determine who are the rightful owners of any property.

3.5 Conclusion

The overwhelming number of property-related cases in Indian courts highlights the urgent need for legal reforms and alternative dispute resolution mechanisms. With millions of cases pending, the inefficiencies of the judicial system contribute to prolonged conflicts that drain financial and emotional resources. This data-driven analysis reinforces the importance of clear legal documentation, awareness of property laws, and proactive estate planning. In the next chapter, we take a closer look at the specific legal provisions governing succession and inheritance in India, providing clarity on how property should be distributed according to the law.

References

- Thomas Reuters, Deccan Chronicle. Millions of land, property cases stuck in courts. August 2016. Available: https://www.deccanchronicle.com/nation/current-affairs/090816/millions-of-land-property-cases-stuck-in-indian-courts.html
- Namita Wahi, Center for Policy Research. Understanding Land Conflict in India and Suggestions for Reform. June 2019. Available: https://cprindia.org/news/7922
- Arunav Kaul, Ahmed Pathan, Harish Narasappa. Daksh report. Deconstructing Delay: Analyses of Data from High Courts and Subordinate Courts. Available: https://dakshindia.org/Daksh_Justice_in_India/19_chapter_01.xhtml
- Madan B Lokur, The Wire. What Is Stopping Our Justice System From Tackling the Cases Pending Before Courts? 12 May 2021. Available: https://thewire.in/law/india-judiciary-pending-cases-supreme-court
- Bloomberg Quint. India's pending court cases on the rise: In charts. 29 September 2020. Available: https://www.bloombergquint.com/law-and-policy/indias-pending-court-cases-on-the-rise-in-charts

Key Takeaways — Chapter 3

Property and land disputes account for approximately 66% of all civil cases in Indian courts, affecting millions of people. The average time to resolve a dispute from filing to final verdict is around 20 years. Legal complexity, lack of digitised land records, and corruption in registration offices are key contributors to the backlog. Wider use of Lok Adalats, simplification of property laws, and digitisation of land records are urgently needed. Every family should maintain clear, current documentation of property ownership to prevent disputes from reaching court.

Chapter 4: Law Related to Succession of Property in India

In this chapter we discuss the main law related to succession and property transfer in India. The main law related to succession is called the Indian Succession Act 1925, which governs the transfer of moveable as well as immoveable property through inheritance or succession upon one's death. It was enacted in British India in 1925, and several amendments have since been made to the law.

4.1 Indian Succession Act 1925

The Indian Succession Act 1925 is an act to consolidate the law applicable to intestate (dying without a will) and testamentary succession (succession where a will is present). The purpose of this law is to present the whole body of statutory law on the subject of wills and succession in a complete form.

The ordinary meaning of the word "succession" is a transmission by law or by the will of the man to one or more persons of the property and transmission rights and obligations of a deceased person.

THE INDIAN SUCCESSION ACT, 1925
ACT NO. 39 OF 1925[1]

[30th September, 1925.]

An Act to consolidate the law applicable to intestate and testamentary succession [2]***.

WHEREAS it is expedient to consolidate the law applicable to intestate and testamentary succession [2]***. It is hereby enacted as follows:—

PART I

PRELIMINARY

1. **Short title.**—This Act may be called the Indian Succession Act, 1925.

2. **Definitions.**—In this Act, unless there is anything repugnant in the subject or context,—

(a) "administrator" means a person appointed by competent authority to administer the estate of a deceased person when there is no executor;

(b) "codicil" means an instrument made in relation to a Will, and explaining, altering or adding to its dispositions, and shall be deemed to form part of the Will;

[3][(bb) "District Judge" means the Judge of a Principal Civil Court of original jurisdiction;]

(c) "executor" means a person to whom the execution of the last Will of a deceased person is, by the testator's appointment, confided;

[4][(cc) "India" means the territory of India excluding the State of Jammu and Kashmir;]

(d) "Indian Christian" means a native of India who is, or in good faith claims to be, of unmixed Asiatic descent and who professes any form of the Christian religion;

Figure: First page of the Indian Succession Act 1925

The law of succession is the law governing the transmission of property vested in a person at his death to some other person or persons.

The act discusses the cases in which a person can die with or without making a will:

- A person dies intestate i.e. without making a will, and how their moveable and immoveable property can be divided among their various heirs starting from the closest relatives such as widow and children.
- Testamentary succession, i.e. where the deceased person has left a will before they died, specifying exactly how their property can be divided and among whom.

4.2 Summary of the Indian succession act

The Indian succession act covers different grounds related to wills and other aspects of succession.

It discusses who can and cannot make a will, what is a valid will, different types of bequests, how an administrator can be appointed, how probate and letters of succession can be granted, how debts, legacies and gifts are to be paid and so on. It also covers different state amendments.

- **Declaration** that this is the **last will** and previous wills are invalid
- **Declaration** that the person is in good health and mind, and is making the will of their **own free choice**
- Names of the **survivors** (wife and children etc.)
- List of **moveable and immoveable property**
- Description of **how the assets are to be divided**
- **Signature** of the person with date
- **Names and Signatures** of two witnesses

Figure: The main components of a will

4.3 Characteristics of a will as per Indian Succession Act

A will can be made for any of the following purposes:

- To dispose of the testator's (the person making the will) property after his death and to appoint an executor
- Appointment of a testamentory guardian
- To cancel or replace a previous will.

The essential characteristics of a will are as follows:

- There must be a legal declaration of the testator's intention
- The declaration must be with respect to the property of the testator
- The declaration must be to the effect that it is to operate after the death of the testator i.e. it should be revocable during the life of the testator.
- It lists the moveable and immoveable assets and states how and among whom the assets are to be divided and in what ratio
- The will must be signed and attested by two witnesses

A will may contain the following components (as a guideline):

- A declaration by the person that this is the last will and all previous wills are invalid
- A declaration that the person is in good health and mind, and is making the will of his own free choice
- Name of the survivors (wife and children)
- Description of the person's moveable and immoveable property
- How the assets are to be divided in in whose names
- Signature of the person with date
- Name and Signature of two witnesses

Before preparing a will, it is necessary to consider the following:

- Whether the testator is competent to draft the will
- Whether the property for which the testator wishes to bequeath is legally correct and which the testator is competent to make a testament to
- Whether the interest the testator wants to create can be created legally
- What conditions which the testator wishes to impose legally can be imposed
- Whether the machinery employed is sufficient and legally sound to satisfy the wishes of the testator

The following formalities have been prescribed by the Indian Succession Act 1925 for a Will:

- The will must be made in writing, except that a soldier or airman in active service or a seafarer at sea, who is not a Hindu, Buddhist, Sikh or Jain, may make an oral will [Section 63, 65 of Indian Succession Act].
- The will must be signed or marked by the testator or any other person in his presence and by his direction [section 63(a)]. The signature should be so placed that it appears that it was intended to give effect to the writing in the form of a will [section 63(b)]. The best place is at the end of writing.
- The will must be attested by two or more persons, each of whom has seen the testator to make his signature or mark or has seen any other person signing in the presence and direction of the testator. Every witness appearing must sign the will in the presence of the testator, but it is not necessary that more than one witness should be present at the same time.

4.4 Things to keep in mind while making arrangements for succession of one's property

Following are some important financial and legal aspects one should keep in mind related to arrangements for their property after one's death:

The choice for a person making arrangements for succession of one's property is between leaving a will or dying intestate. A valid will ensures that a testator can determine what happens to our property after his death. If one does not make a will, i.e. one dies intestate, the law of the state will determine how one's property will be distributed to whom and in what proportions and the person has no choice in the matter. Without a will, assets and belongings will be distributed on death according to the law of intestacy. The intestacy laws benefit blood relatives in the order of proximity, but charities and close friends get nothing.

In order to prepare one's will, one needs to approach a solicitor. Any solicitor can prepare a will. The solicitor fees can vary from as less as Rs 50000 to 200000 depending on the following factors:

- Size of the estate
- The complexity of the will itself

It is advisable to confirm in advance with the solicitor how much would be the legal cost. Alternatively, a person may choose not to use a solicitor and draft a will by himself. Similarly, a person may choose whether to register his will at the sub-registrar's office or not.

The things to keep in mind after drafting one's will are as follows:

- Once a will is executed (written, signed and attested by two witnesses) it takes a legal form.

- It can then be kept in a safe place by the testator, to be opened after his or her death.
- It can also be kept at a sub registrar's office (what is called a "registered will") for safety and record keeping.
- Note: Since the will may not be seen till after the funeral is over, it is a good idea to tell one's family and proposed executors about one's wishes in terms of the manner of one's funeral and organ donation, since this cannot be delayed
- A person may, before one's death, tell one's family members that he or she has signed a will and deposited for safekeeping in a probate court or bank

When someone dies, the partner or close relatives have to deal with a multitude of practical matters as well as coping with their emotions. In the short term:

- the death must be registered
- arrangements should be made for the funeral
- the immediate day to day expenses of the dependents must be provided for, after which the affairs of the deceased person must be settled.

This means someone must take charge of his/her property, personal possessions, debts, business and so forth, which the law calls by the term "the deceased's estate".

No charge is to be levied for a medical certificate if the death was due to natural causes. One must register the death within five days with the concerned Registrar of births, marriages and deaths. The death is recorded in a register of deaths and a certified copy of the entry is called "the death certificate". Several copies of the death certificate need to be prepared for use in different places.

4.5 Some points related to the affairs of the deceased person

Arranging for the funeral: Funeral directors should provide one with the price lists and written estimates. Whoever arranges the funeral is responsible for payment. If the deceased left enough assets or cash, one may be able to claim reimbursement out of the estate for reasonable funeral expenses.

Joint bank accounts: Personal accounts are frozen on death. Joint accounts can be operated provided that both the account holders are not required to sign every cheque. One can operate a joint account provided it needs a single signature.

The deceased's papers: In order to find out of there is a will, one needs to go through the personal papers left by the deceased, check with his or her bank along with the past and present solicitors whether they hold his will. It might also have been deposited in the safe custody of the registry.

Bank direct debits, standing orders and credit cards: One should check all direct debit mandates and standing orders. These cease on death if paid through a bank account in the deceased's sole name. One should make sure that all credit cards are returned with notice of death to the card companies, in order to avoid fraudulent misuse.

The personal representatives of the deceased: These are the people who are the official representatives of the deceased to take charge of an estate:

- To take charge of the deceased's property
- To pay outstanding debts and taxes
- To ascertain which persons are entitled to what is left
- To ensure that beneficiaries are given their proper share

4.5 Format of a sample will

The format of a sample will is as follows:

I, <name of testator>, son of <father's name>, aged <age in years>, resident of <address of testator>, declare this to be my last will and testament. This will cancels all my prior wills made by me.

I am in good health and possess a good mind. This will was made independently by me. No one has influenced or compelled me to make this will.

I hereby appoint <name of executor>, as the sole executor of this will.

My wife's name is <name of wife>. We have <number of children> children, whose names are as follows:

1.

2.

I have the following immovable and movable property:

1. A flat in the address ____

2. Jewelry, shares in various companies, cash and cash in bank accounts.

I declare that all the above assets are owned by me, and I have full authority over these assets.

I entrust all my movable and immovable properties to the following persons in the following ways

1. I give my bank account to my wife

2. I give my flat in the name of my son

(   )

Testator's signature

Date

Signed by the testator as a last will in our presence. We have fully understood and approved the material and have signed our names as witnesses in the presence of the testator and in the presence of each other.

Name and signature of witnesses:

1.(name and signature of witness)

2. (name and signature of witness)

4.6 Understanding the testator's intention

To ascertain the intention of the testator while making a will, the court is concerned with three distinct questions:

- What words has the testator used to express his intention
- What is the meaning of such words in relation to the persons and the things described; and
- What is the meaning of the words in relation to the disposition of such property among the donee(s)

When the intention of the testator has been discovered, the next enquiry by the court should be to ascertain whether there is any rule preventing the intention from taking effect and how the intention can be effectuated (Halisbury law).

4.7 Probate of a will

Probate is the legal procedure in which the deceased person's property is examined and evaluated, claims against the estate are paid and the remaining property is distributed:

- to the heirs if there is a will or
- according to intestacy / state law if no will is present

Probate is also the name given to the petition to the court for granting the authority to an executor to execute the will of a testator.

Probate of a will, when granted, establishes the will from the death of the testator and renders valid all intermediate acts of the executor as such.

Probate is conclusive as to the genuineness of the will and appointment of executors.

Once probate is granted, no suit will lie for a declaration that the testator was not of a sound mind.

Probate is conclusive as to the representative title of the executor against the debtors of the deceased and gives complete indemnity to them, as per Section 273 of ISA 1925.

As the executor derives his title under the will and all the properties of the testator vest in him immediately on the death of the testator, on the grant of probate, all his intermediate acts in connection with the estate are validated [AIR 1956 Mod 274]. This section enacts that the vesting takes place on the taking of probate but relates back to the time of the testator's death and to the estate which then belonged to him. Under Section 221 of ISA 1925, in the case of an administrator only those acts which are beneficial to the estate and validated by the grant are validated.

A probate petition should contain the following details:

- Details of the deceased and their legal heirs
- Details of the will, including date and circumstances of death
- Details of the property of the deceased
- Statement that the petitioners are the sole heirs as per the will and undertake to pay the duties
- Prayer to grant probate
- Affidavit of the petitioners

4.8 Proving genuineness of a will and suspicious circumstances

To prove the genuineness of the will in a court of law, the propounder must prove five things:

- The testamentary capacity of the testator, i.e., of the person making the will
- The testamentary nature of the instrument, i.e., that the will does not dispose of any property in present but only on the death of the executant
- The testator's knowledge of the contents of the instrument and his approval of the same.
- The absence of undue influence, fraud etc.
- Due execution by the testator and its attestation by witnesses as required by law.

The list of suspicious circumstances surrounding a will can include the following:

- Signature of the testator may be shaky and doubtful.
- The condition of the testator's mind may appear to be feeble and debilitated.
- Mental capacity of the testator may be doubtful.
- The dispositions made in the will may appear to be unnatural, improbable or unfair.
- The will may otherwise indicate that the said dispositions may not be the result of the testator's free will of mind.
- Exercise of undue influence, fraud or coercion can be shown in respect of execution of will.
- the propounder of the will themselves takes a prominent part in the execution of the will which confers on them substantial benefit.

4.8a Validity of a will obtained by coercion or undue influence

If it is proved that a will is obtained by dubious means such as coercion, fraud or undue influence, such a will is ruled to be invalid. Some instances include the following:

- **Coercion**: Whatever destroys the free agency of the testator constitutes coercion. If actual force was used to compel the testator to make the will and all the formalities are complied with, yet the will is void [1 Cox 355]. Examples of coercion include threat to suicide by any of the parties, in order to compel the testator to include them in their will.

- **Undue influence**: Undue influence is the improper use of power or trust in a way that deprives a person of free will and substitutes another's objective [Black's Law Dictionary: 8th Edition]. It is any kind of influence that takes away the free agency of the testator.

- **Unsound mind**: If at the time of making the will the testator is proven to have unsound mind, that will is proven to be invalid. Unsoundness of mind may be occasioned by physical infirmity or advancing years as distinguished from mental derangement and the resulting defeat of intelligence may be the cause of incapacity, but the intelligence must be reduced to such an extent that the proposed testator does not appreciate the testamentary act in all its bearings. Old age or the near approach of death at any age, lend strength to the suggestion that the testator had proper knowledge of the contents of the will [Williams, Law of Wills pp. 20-21].

To prove a will is valid, the propounder of the will has to show that the will was signed by the testator, that he was at the relevant time in a sound disposing state of mind, that he understood the nature and the effect of the dispositions, that he had signed in the presence of two witnesses who attested it in his presence and in the presence of each other. Once these elements are established, the onus which rests on the propounder is discharged [Surendra Pal v Dr. Sarswati AIR 1974 SC 1999].

4.9 Example of a Probate Petition

If the deceased leaves a will that the executors name, the executor must apply to the Probate Division of the High Court for the grant of probate. If the will is made in duplicate, both parts must be filed on a petition for probate. If there is no will, the estate's administrators will be given letters of administration by the same probate division as the next of kin.

A sample petition for probate is as follows:

In the court of jurisdiction of ____

Probate Case Number __ *of* __ *<year>*

In the case of

*Mr.*__ *<Petitioner Name>*

Resident of ___ *(petitioner)*

versus

State (Respondent)

Probate petition under section 276 of the Indian Succession Act on behalf of the petitioners in respect of the will of the testator executed on <date> of the <deceased name>, son of <father's name> filed on behalf of <>.

The side of the petitioners i.e. <name of the petitioners>.

1. ___, son of ___, resident of ___, hereinafter referred to as deceased, who was a Hindu governed by the Hindu Succession Act, died on ___ at ___, which was his place of residence. A copy of the death certificate issued by the Sub Registrar of Births and Deaths is given as Annexure A.

2. At the time of death, the age of the deceased was approximately ___ years. During his life time, the deceased ___ dated ___ in respect of movable and immovable property, duly executed will.

3. That at the time of death, the deceased has left behind the following legal heirs:

i) Name, address, age, relationship

ii) Name, address, age, relationship

iii) Name, address, age, relationship

4. That before his death, the deceased executed a will on date _____ in favor of ___ and ___

5. That the deceased was competent to draft the will on date ___, being the owner of the property in _____

6. It is submitted that through the said will, the said property has been bequeathed to the relatives of the deceased in the following manner:

i)

ii)

iii)

7. That after the death of _____ the petitioner became the sole executor/legal heir of the deceased testator as per the will in respect of the above mentioned property.

8. The deceased was living in _____ location, died on ___ date ___.

Also the property left by the deceased was located at ___, which is under the jurisdiction of this Hon'ble Court.

9. This pertains to the affidavit of _____ dated _____, who is one of the witnesses.

10. That the value of the property of the deceased beyond the State limits of _____ does not exceed Rs.____

11. To the knowledge of the petitioner, no application for the said Will has been made in any High Court or other District Court.

12. That the petitioner undertakes to pay the fees due for the grant of probate.

Prayer

The petitioner therefore most respectfully prays that in the interest of justice in the facts and circumstances of the case, probate may be granted in respect of the will executed by late _____ in favor of the petitioner.

For such other order/relief/direction, this Hon'ble Court may be appropriate and appropriate also to pass in favor of the petitioners.

Affidavit

I, _____, son of _____, age____, resident of _____, hereby solemnly confirm and declare that:

1. That I am Petitioner 1 and am well aware of the facts of the case.

2. That the facts given in the petition have been drafted by our counsel under our directions which are all correct.

(Signature of petitioner)

Location:

Date:

4.10 Conclusion

Succession laws in India, while comprehensive, are often misunderstood or misapplied, leading to unnecessary disputes. The Indian Succession Act and other related laws offer clear guidelines on inheritance, whether through wills or intestate succession. However, the complexity of these laws necessitates careful legal planning to prevent conflicts. As we move to the next chapter, we will explore the laws governing the transfer of property, a critical aspect for individuals and families managing their assets effectively.

Key Takeaways — Chapter 4

The Indian Succession Act 1925 governs how property passes on death, both with and without a will. A valid will must be in writing, signed by the testator, and attested by two witnesses. Dying without a will means the state decides how your assets are distributed, which may not reflect your wishes. A will can be challenged on grounds of coercion, undue influence, or unsound mind — careful drafting and registration provide important protection. Registering the will at the sub-registrar's office and informing your executor of its location are vital steps.

Chapter 5: Law Related to Transfer of Property in India

The main law related to transfer of property between living persons in India is called Transfer of Property Act, which consolidates the law in India related to property transfers. The act was made in British India in 1882 and has survived in independent India with a few modifications.

> THE TRANSFER OF PROPERTY ACT, 1882
> ACT NO. 4 OF 1882
> [17th February, 1882.]
>
> An Act to amend the law relating to the Transfer of Property by act of Parties.
>
> **Preamble.**—WHEREAS it is expedient to define and amend certain parts of the law relating to the transfer of property by act of parties; It is hereby enacted as follows:—
>
> CHAPTER I
> PRELIMINARY
>
> **1. Short title.**—This Act may becalled the Transfer of Property Act, 1882.
>
> **Commencements.**—It shallcome into force on the first day of July, 1882.
>
> **Extent.**—[Itextends² in the first instance to the whole of India. except ³[the territories which, immediately before the 1st November, 1956, were comprised in Part B States or in the States of], Bombay, Punjab and Delhi.]
>
> ⁴[But this Act or any part thereof may by ⁵notification in the Official Gazette be extended to the whole or any part of ⁶[the said territories] by the State Government concerned.]
>
> ⁷[And any State Government may, ⁸*** from time to time, by notification in the Official Gazette, exempt, either retrospectively or prospectively, any part of the territories administered by such State Government from all or any of the following provisions, namely:—
>
> Sections 54, paragraphs 2 and 3, 59, 107 and 123.]

Figure: First page of the Transfer of Property Act 1882

5.1 Introduction to the Transfer of Property Act

The Transfer of Property Act states the conditions and procedure following which a property can get transferred from one person to another. It discusses the different modes of transfer of property including sales, mortgages, leases, exchange and gifts.

In this act, property refers to both moveable as well as immoveable property. Transfer of property, according to the act, is defined as conveying a property to himself or another living person, including a company or group of individuals, in present or future. The rights, interest, ownership and/or possession of the property can be transferred.

As per the act, any person who is mentally competent and fulfills the other conditions for making a contract can transfer property to another, provided they own the property or are authorized to transfer it. They can transfer it orally or in writing, themselves or by hiring a competent lawyer.

5.2 Conditions for the transfer of property under Transfer of Property Act

The conditions for transfer are as follows:

- The transfer must be between two living persons
- The property being transferred should be transferable. It should not have any circumstances in which it cannot be transferred, such as chance of a heir apparent succeeding to an estate. It should not be a common asset belonging to all, such as the air or sea, that cannot be transferred.
- The person making the transfer should own the property or be competent to transfer it.
- The transfer should be done via a valid method such as sale, exchange, mortgage, lease or gift.
- The transfer cannot be in opposition to the rule of perpetuity. E.g. there should be no condition in the transfer that occurs

after infinite time or the lifetime of any of the persons involved.

5.3 Types of Transfers Under Transfer of Property Act

The Transfer of Property act describes different ways in which property can be transferred. For each of these, it describes the transfer and the rights and duties of the parties to the transfer.

The different types of transfer described in the Transfer of Property act are as follows:

- Sale of property: Sale means a transfer of ownership upon a price paid or promised.
- Mortgage of immoveable property: This refers to the transfer of interest in immoveable property as a security for a loan. The act contains detailed instructions on the rights and liabilities of a mortgager and mortgagee, how the mortgage can be redeemed, issues such as foreclosure of a mortgage, how a receiver can be appointed and so on.
- Lease of immoveable property: This is the transfer of the rights to enjoy a property for a specified time and upon regular payment of an amount or rent.
- Exchange: This is when two persons mutually transfer the ownership of one thing for another or for money only, it is called an exchange.
- Gift: Gift is the transfer of moveable or immoveable property by one party, called the donor, to another party called the donee, voluntarily and without any consideration, and accepted by the donee party.
- Actionable claim: Transfer of actionable claim means transfer of property upon a claim such as debt, from the

debtor to the one they are in debt to, or who has a legally enforceable claim against them.

For each of the above types of transfers, the act lays down the procedure and defines the rights and liabilities of the parties to the transfer.

5.4 Conclusion

Property transfer laws provide a legal framework for the sale, lease, mortgage, and gifting of assets, ensuring smooth transactions and reducing disputes. However, a lack of legal awareness often results in fraudulent transactions and ownership conflicts. Understanding these laws is crucial for protecting property rights and ensuring legally valid transfers. In the next chapter, we will discuss the procedure for fighting property disputes in court, guiding individuals through the legal process when conflicts arise.

Key Takeaways — Chapter 5

The Transfer of Property Act 1882 governs how property moves between living persons through sale, mortgage, lease, exchange, or gift. Any transfer must involve legally competent parties, transferable property, and a recognised legal method. Gifting property without legal safeguards can be misused, as several high-profile family disputes have demonstrated. Understanding the rights and duties of all parties in a transaction is critical to avoiding future disputes. Always insist on registered, written agreements for any property transaction, regardless of how close the other party may be.

Chapter 6: Procedure for Fighting Property Court Cases

A property court case, as we have seen earlier, typically takes several years in Indian courts. The initial case may be filed at the district court or some lower court. In case of an unfavorable verdict, some of the parties may appeal in higher courts such as the high court or supreme court.

Most family related property court cases are succession related i.e. when the patriarch or matriarch of the family has died leaving some property and the children are fighting to divide it among themselves. In that case, they may be related to a will, if it exists, or multiple copies of the will, or in some cases there may be no will at all. Most of such cases would be governed under the Indian Succession Act and would be related to getting a probate or letters of administration of the will. Even within will related succession court cases, there may be a variety: cases related to moveable property left in the will, immoveable property, or both.

There might also be family cases related to other things than succession, for example if the patriarch is old but not died yet and the sons are fighting over who will manage the assets of the family business.

6.1 Court Procedure for probate and other property cases

The court procedure for probating a will generally includes the following steps (note that the exact procedure may vary from state to state):

- **Submission**: Petitioners file the probate application at the court in the prescribed format, along with original copies of the will, death certificate, affidavit and court fees.
- **Verification**: Court receives the probate application and verifies details.
- **Publication**: Court directs to publish in newspapers a notice inviting members of the public and next of kin to file objections. It also directs to send notification letters to the next of kin to appear in the court.
- **Issuance**: If there is no objection, the court issues the probate and letters of administration.
- **Upon Objection**: If there is an objection, the normal court procedure takes place. This includes filing of arguments and evidence, cross examination etc. After examining evidence and arguments, the court issues its judgment regarding the grant of probate.

For property cases other than probate of a will, a similar procedure is applicable, except that parts related to the will are not used.

In the following subsections we share some important things to keep in mind when fighting the cases.

6.2 Choosing a good lawyer for fighting the court cases

Not all lawyers are the same. Some genuinely help their clients resolve property matters efficiently, while others deliberately prolong cases to keep the legal fees flowing. Understanding how property lawyers operate is key to making informed decisions.

The Good Lawyers:

- They focus on **quick resolution** and advise on alternative dispute resolution (ADR) methods.

- They provide **clear legal guidance** and keep clients updated on case progress.
- They discourage unnecessary litigation and help negotiate settlements.

The Bad Lawyers:

- They intentionally **delay cases** to keep charging clients year after year.
- They make **false promises** about quick verdicts to extract higher fees.
- They work in collaboration with the opposing party, secretly undermining their client.

One important strategy for court cases is to get a good and competent lawyer whom we can trust to fight the court cases.

One should engage a lawyer who is competent and has prior experience in dealing with such cases in his or her career. We should make sure the lawyer keeps themselves abreast of current knowledge in law including recent judgments, is comfortable with technology such as email and remote hearings.

Considering that remote hearings and e-filings have become more common nowadays with the Covid-19 pandemic and are here to stay even after the pandemic is over, we should make sure that the lawyer too should be comfortable with this.

The most important quality in a good lawyer is that they should listen to the client and be ready to act as per the client's instructions. They should not have the attitude that they know better than the client, or that they always know what is best and their decisions cannot be questioned. The best lawyers are usually humble, open minded and respect the fact that the client knows best about his or her own case.

6.3 Managing one's lawyer

We should try to skillfully manage the lawyer during the conduct of the case, including negotiating the fees in advance, giving proper incentives and so on. We should also try to be friendly with the lawyer and not pick up fights with them over petty issues. If we decide to change the lawyer, we should try to do so amicably and without fighting.

We can also use our lawyer in efficient ways, such as sending them to appear for court dates and avoid unnecessary travel for ourselves.

6.4 Changing one's lawyer

One should not be attached to any one lawyer and be ready to change one's lawyer if the need arises, for example if the current lawyer is no longer able to effectively represent our case.

The normal procedure is to file a new "wakalatnama" for the new lawyer at the court, stating that this lawyer will be representing this case from now on.

As per the Indian laws, the existing lawyer cannot stop any client from changing their lawyer, even if they do not provide a "No Objection Certificate".

Having said that, it is also not a good practice to change lawyers too frequently during the case. Having chosen a lawyer, we should not have undue expectations on them and give them some time to prove themselves. We should also try to be amicable while changing the lawyer.

6.5 Middlemen and Brokers in Property Disputes

Property brokers and middlemen often act as **power brokers** in disputes, facilitating deals between warring family members or between buyers and sellers. While some work honestly, others exploit people desperate to resolve their cases quickly.

How Middlemen Operate:

- They promise quick settlements but often **inflate the deal value** to extract their cut.

- Some work as **informants for land grabbers**, alerting them to vulnerable properties.

- Others act as **fixers in courts**, using bribes to influence property judgments.

Tip: Be cautious while dealing with property middlemen. If you must use a broker, ensure all agreements are documented and legally vetted.

6.6 Corruption in Land Records & Registry Offices

One of the biggest challenges in property disputes is dealing with corrupt officials at land registry offices. These officials can alter ownership records, delay crucial documents, or demand bribes for routine work.

Common Scams in Land Records Offices:

- **Duplicate Title Deeds:** Fraudsters create fake ownership documents and sell disputed land.

- **Forged Signatures:** Some officials illegally transfer land ownership by forging signatures.

- **Deliberate File Loss:** Important documents go "missing" unless a bribe is paid.

Tip: Always verify land records through online portals where available (e.g., Dharani for Telangana, Bhulekh for UP). Regularly check if your property details have been altered.

6.7 Handling finances for fighting property court cases

An important part of any court case is handling one's finances properly. If not properly planned and budgeted in advance, the costs including the lawyer's fees, cost of hiring new lawyers, cost of filing additional cases, travel related to cases etc. may spiral out of control.

Therefore, it is important to first estimate the budget by asking our friends and acquaintances who have dealt with similar cases. We can also research on the internet or on forums such as lawrato.com where one can get advice from lawyers on specific aspects of the law.

Having estimated our budget for the case, we should figure out how to arrange our finances to pay for it. We should also take into account that the case can drag for a longer time and may lead to multiple related cases rather than just a single case. Even if we cannot estimate a fixed number given all kinds of varying costs, we should budget for a certain approximate sum every year the case runs,

In times when we have to make finance related decisions, such as if our lawyer advises us to file an additional case or go for a strategy that costs us money, we should do a proper cost benefit analysis before deciding to allocate extra funds.

The same goes for how to pay the lawyer's fees. We should negotiate paying them in installments rather than the entire fee at once, and also make it dependent on how long the case runs.

6.8 The art of cross examination

Sometimes, we may be cross examined by the opposite party, during the conduct of the case. Or else, we may have to advise our own lawyer on how to cross examine the opposite party and what questions to ask them. It is important to prepare properly for such an eventuality. We should act as our own devil's advocate and prepare a list of questions as well as the opposite party's probable answers to all such questions. We should even practice the cross-examination session with a friend or simply in front of a mirror. We should not take it lightly but try our best to give the prepared answers as per our strategy so as not to weaken our case. Similarly, we should prepare the questions for the opposite party based on a close analysis of their position and how best to weaken their case. We should go over the questions carefully with our lawyer beforehand.

6.9 The Scam of Deliberate Court Delays

The judicial system is slow, but deliberate delays in property cases often result from legal tactics used by unethical lawyers and litigants. Some common tricks include:

- **Repeated Adjournments:** Lawyers cite vague reasons to postpone hearings.
- **Changing Legal Representation:** Defendants frequently change lawyers to reset proceedings.
- **Filing Counter-Cases:** To confuse the legal process, multiple lawsuits are filed on the same property.

Tip: Stay actively involved in your case, attend hearings, and insist on regular updates from your lawyer.

6.10 How to Avoid Getting Exploited in Property Cases

While it's difficult to completely avoid the legal maze, taking the right steps can help you avoid unnecessary financial and emotional strain.

Choose a Lawyer Wisely

- Look for lawyers with a **proven track record** in property litigation.
- Avoid lawyers who **guarantee quick results**—they may be lying.
- Negotiate fees **upfront** to prevent unexpected costs.

Digitally Safeguard Property Documents

- Store **scanned copies** of all documents in a secure cloud storage.
- Regularly check **land ownership records** online.

Explore Alternative Dispute Resolution (ADR)

- Mediation and arbitration can **resolve disputes faster** than courts.
- Many courts encourage **Lok Adalats** to settle property disputes amicably.

Stay Aware of Legal Time Limits

- Property laws have **statutes of limitation**—delaying legal action could weaken your case.
- Seek legal advice **before a dispute escalates**.

6.11 Conclusion

Litigation over property disputes is often a long and complex process, requiring careful legal strategy and financial planning. Understanding court procedures, the importance of legal representation, and the potential for mediation can help individuals navigate disputes more effectively. Given the high cost and emotional toll of prolonged litigation, alternative resolution methods should be considered wherever possible. In the following chapter, we will examine the role of women in property disputes, shedding light on their legal rights and the challenges they face in claiming their inheritance.

Key Takeaways — Chapter 6

Choosing a competent, trustworthy lawyer from the outset is the single most important decision in a property dispute. Negotiate fees upfront, arrange instalment payments, and stay actively involved in your case's progress. Watch for deliberate delay tactics — repeated adjournments, frequent lawyer changes by the opposite party, and counter-cases filed to confuse proceedings. Maintain digital backups of all property documents and regularly verify land records through official online portals. Wherever possible, explore mediation or arbitration before committing to full litigation.

Chapter 7: The Role of Women in Property Disputes

Property rights for women in India have long been a contentious issue, shaped by historical customs, legal reforms, and social attitudes. While laws have evolved significantly, many women still face obstacles in claiming their rightful share of family property. In this chapter, we will explore the changing landscape of women's property rights, landmark legal cases, and the ongoing challenges that women encounter in inheritance disputes.

7.1 The Evolution of Women's Property Rights in India

For centuries, Indian society followed a patriarchal inheritance system, where property was largely passed down to male heirs. Women, especially daughters, were often excluded from ancestral wealth. However, with legal reforms, particularly after independence, the status of women's property rights has changed significantly.

Key Legal Reforms:

- The Hindu Succession Act, 1956: This law initially granted limited property rights to women, favoring sons over daughters.

- The Hindu Succession (Amendment) Act, 2005: A landmark change that gave daughters equal rights as sons in ancestral property.

- Muslim Personal Law: Under Sharia law, women inherit property but receive a smaller share compared to men.

- Indian Succession Act, 1925: Governs inheritance for Christians and Parsis, granting equal rights to male and female heirs.

Despite these progressive changes, the implementation remains inconsistent, with societal and familial resistance still prevalent.

7.2 Landmark Supreme Court Judgments on Women's Property Rights

Indian courts have played a crucial role in strengthening women's inheritance rights. Some of the most influential Supreme Court rulings include:

- Vineeta Sharma v. Rakesh Sharma (2020): The Supreme Court ruled that daughters have equal rights to ancestral property, regardless of whether their father was alive before the 2005 amendment. Reference: https://indiankanoon.org/doc/67965481/

- Danamma v. Amar Singh (2018): The court clarified that daughters born before 2005 were also entitled to equal shares in ancestral property. Reference: https://lawbhoomi.com/danamma-vs-amar-singh

- Prakash v. Phulavati (2015): Initially ruled that the 2005 amendment applied only to cases where the father was alive after 2005, later overruled by the Vineeta Sharma judgment. Reference: https://indiankanoon.org/doc/143363828/

These judgments have reaffirmed that gender cannot be a barrier to inheritance rights in modern India.

7.3 The Challenges Women Face in Claiming Property Rights

Despite favourable laws, many women struggle to exercise their property rights due to:

- Social Pressure: Families often discourage daughters from claiming property to maintain harmony.
- Emotional Guilt: Women are made to feel guilty for demanding their rightful share.
- Lack of Awareness: Many women, especially in rural areas, are unaware of their legal rights.
- Legal Loopholes: Property is sometimes transferred to male relatives before the daughter can claim her share.
- Threats and Intimidation: In extreme cases, women face violence or social ostracization for pursuing their claims.

7.4 Steps Women Can Take to Secure Their Property Rights

Women must take proactive steps to protect their inheritance rights:

1. Get Property Registered: Ensure that your name is included in property documents.
2. Keep Legal Documents Safe: Maintain copies of wills, land records, and family agreements.
3. Seek Legal Advice Early: Consult a property lawyer as soon as a dispute arises.
4. Use Mediation When Possible: Family mediation can sometimes resolve disputes faster than courts.
5. Know Your Rights: Stay informed about property laws relevant to your religion and state.

7.5 Conclusion

Despite legal advancements, women in India continue to face significant challenges in asserting their property rights due to social pressures, lack of awareness, and deeply ingrained patriarchal norms. Landmark court judgments have strengthened women's inheritance rights, but more awareness and enforcement are needed to ensure equality. As we move forward, we will explore property disputes involving Non-Resident Indians (NRIs) and overseas Indians, who face unique challenges in managing and protecting their assets from fraud and encroachment.

Key Takeaways — Chapter 7

The Hindu Succession (Amendment) Act 2005 granted daughters equal rights to ancestral property as sons, a historic reform. The Supreme Court's Vineeta Sharma judgment (2020) reinforced these rights retroactively, regardless of when the father died. Despite the law, many women face social pressure, guilt, and intimidation when claiming their inheritance. Women should ensure their names appear on property documents, keep certified copies of all relevant records, and consult a lawyer promptly when a dispute arises. Legal awareness is the most powerful tool available to women asserting their property rights.

Chapter 8: Property Disputes in NRIs and Overseas Indians

Property disputes involving Non-Resident Indians (NRIs) and overseas Indians are particularly complex due to geographical distance, legal loopholes, and the high incidence of fraud. Many NRIs inherit or invest in property in India, only to find themselves entangled in legal battles over encroachment, illegal occupation, or fraudulent transfers. This chapter explores the major issues NRIs face, landmark legal cases, and ways to safeguard property rights from afar.

8.1 Why NRIs Face More Property Issues in India?

Owning property in India while living abroad can be challenging. NRIs often encounter problems such as:

- **Encroachment by Relatives or Strangers:** Unscrupulous relatives or tenants illegally occupying the property.
- **Fraudulent Sales:** Properties are sometimes sold using forged documents, leaving the real owner unaware until legal action is required to reclaim them.
- **Power of Attorney (PoA) Abuse:** Trusted individuals misusing their authority to transfer property.
- **Legal Complexity:** Navigating different state laws and slow judicial processes.
- **Land Mafia and Corruption:** Organized groups targeting vacant NRI properties.

Due to these factors, many NRIs struggle to claim their rightful ownership or regain control of disputed assets.

8.2 Legal Provisions to Safeguard NRI Property

India has laws to protect NRI property owners, but enforcement remains a challenge. Some key provisions include:

- **Transfer of Property Act, 1882:** Ensures rightful ownership and protects against unauthorized transfers.
- **Specific Relief Act, 1963:** Allows NRIs to reclaim illegally occupied property.
- **Hindu Succession Act, 1956 (Amended 2005):** Ensures daughters (even NRIs) have equal rights in ancestral property.
- **RERA (Real Estate Regulatory Authority) Act, 2016:** Helps NRIs in cases of fraud by builders and developers.
- **Adverse Possession Law:** If a property is illegally occupied for 12 years, the occupant can claim ownership. This is a serious risk for NRI properties.

8.3 How NRIs Can Protect Their Property

To avoid long legal battles, NRIs should take proactive steps:

Use Power of Attorney (PoA) Wisely

NRIs often give PoA to relatives or lawyers to manage property transactions. However, this can be misused.

- Always give a **limited PoA** instead of a general PoA.

- Specify the exact powers being granted.
- Register PoA with the Indian consulate and local authorities.

Digitally Monitor Property

- Register property online with state revenue departments.
- Use digital land records portals to check ownership status.
- Hire a property management firm for regular updates.

Periodic Visits & Legal Documentation

- Visit India periodically to ensure the property is maintained.
- Keep original documents, title deeds, and tax records safe.
- Register any tenancy agreements with the local authorities.

File a Police Complaint if Required

If property encroachment occurs, NRIs can file complaints under:

- **Section 441 IPC** (Criminal trespass)
- **Section 420 IPC** (Fraud and cheating)
- **Section 406 IPC** (Criminal breach of trust)
- **Section 503 IPC** (Criminal intimidation)

8.4 Steps to Reclaim Encroached Property

If an NRI finds their property illegally occupied, they should:

1. **Hire a local property lawyer** to send a legal notice.
2. **File a civil suit for possession** under the Specific Relief Act.
3. **Seek police assistance** for criminal trespass complaints.

4. **Use fast-track courts** to speed up the case.
5. **Sell or lease out unused property** to reduce the risk of encroachment.

8.5 The Role of NRI Property Cells

Many Indian states now have dedicated NRI property cells to handle disputes:

- **Punjab NRI Affairs Cell:** Resolves land disputes involving overseas Punjabis.
- **Delhi NRI Cell:** Handles property-related fraud cases.
- **Maharashtra NRI Wing:** Assists in real estate fraud investigations.
- **Kerala NRI Commission:** Handles inheritance and land issues.

These government initiatives offer hope for NRIs dealing with property fraud.

8.6 Conclusion

NRIs often struggle to manage property disputes from abroad, facing issues like illegal occupation, fraud, and legal complexities. Ensuring proper documentation, legal representation, and vigilance over property records is essential for protecting their assets. The increasing number of NRI property disputes highlights the need for better legal safeguards and efficient dispute resolution mechanisms. In the next chapter, we will discuss the role of alternative dispute resolution (ADR) in settling property conflicts without prolonged litigation.

Key Takeaways — Chapter 8

NRIs face heightened property risks due to distance: encroachment, fraudulent sales, and Power of Attorney (PoA) misuse are common. Adverse possession law means that property left unmonitored for 12 years can potentially be claimed by an illegal occupant. Use a limited, specific PoA rather than a general one, and register it with Indian consular authorities. Digital land record portals, periodic visits to India, and a trusted local property management firm are essential safeguards. Punjab, Delhi, Maharashtra, and Kerala have dedicated NRI property cells to assist with disputes.

Chapter 9: Alternative Dispute Resolution (ADR) for Property Disputes

Property disputes in India can stretch for decades, draining finances, emotions, and relationships. Litigation is often a long and exhausting battle, but it is not the only option. Alternative Dispute Resolution (ADR) methods such as **mediation, arbitration, and Lok Adalats** offer a faster and more efficient way to resolve conflicts. This chapter explores how ADR works, its advantages over traditional litigation, and real-life examples of families who successfully used it to settle disputes.

9.1 Why ADR is Better Than Litigation in Property Disputes

Going to court is often the default choice for people involved in property disputes, but it is not always the best option. Litigation can be:

- **Time-Consuming:** Cases can last 10–20 years or more.
- **Expensive:** Lawyer fees, court fees, and travel expenses add up.
- **Emotionally Draining:** Family members often become bitter enemies.
- **Unpredictable:** Court judgments can be delayed or appealed indefinitely.

ADR, on the other hand, offers a **quicker, cost-effective, and relationship-friendly** alternative.

9.2 Types of Alternative Dispute Resolution (ADR) in India

There are several ADR mechanisms available for resolving property disputes:

Mediation – A Middle Ground Solution

- Mediation involves a neutral third party (mediator) who helps both sides reach a **mutually agreeable solution**.
- The mediator does not **impose a decision** but facilitates dialogue between disputing parties.
- **Court-ordered mediation** is becoming common in Indian courts to reduce the backlog of cases.
- **Example:** Two brothers fighting over ancestral property resolved their case in 6 months through mediation, avoiding a 10-year court battle.

Arbitration – A Legally Binding Agreement

- Arbitration is **similar to a private court**, where an arbitrator (often a retired judge or senior lawyer) hears both sides and delivers a legally binding decision.
- This method is **faster than regular courts** but still allows parties to present evidence and arguments.
- **Example:** A property developer and a homeowner settled a land encroachment dispute within a year using arbitration instead of a decade-long court case.

Lok Adalats – Quick and Legally Enforceable Resolutions

- Lok Adalats (People's Courts) resolve disputes **through compromise** and **are legally binding**.

- They are **organized by legal services authorities** and are commonly used for land and tenancy disputes.
- **Example:** A farmer facing illegal occupation of his land got it resolved in one day through a Lok Adalat instead of waiting 15 years in court.

Online Dispute Resolution (ODR) – The Future of Property Disputes

- With advancements in technology, property disputes can now be resolved online through **digital mediation and arbitration platforms**.
- Some courts in India have started **virtual Lok Adalats** to speed up resolutions.
- **Example:** An NRI settled an inheritance dispute with his cousins in India via an online mediation platform, saving years of legal trouble.

9.3 When to Choose ADR Over Litigation?

Not every property dispute is suited for ADR. Here's when you should consider ADR:

- **When both parties are open to negotiation** and willing to compromise.
- **If you want a faster resolution** instead of a long legal battle.
- **To preserve family relationships** in cases of inheritance disputes.
- **If the issue involves property division** rather than criminal fraud.

ADR may not be effective in cases where:

- One party is **completely unwilling to cooperate**.
- There is **criminal fraud, forgery, or illegal land grabbing** involved.
- The dispute has **already escalated into violent threats**.

9.4 The Process of ADR in Property Disputes

Step 1: Selecting the Right ADR Method

- Mediation: If you want a negotiated settlement.
- Arbitration: If you need a legally binding but faster decision.
- Lok Adalat: If both parties are open to compromise.
- Online Dispute Resolution: If you want a digital, time-saving option.

Step 2: Engaging a Neutral Third Party

- Contact a **certified mediator/arbitrator** from legal service authorities or private organizations.
- In court-referred mediation, the court assigns a mediator.

Step 3: Conducting the ADR Process

- Both parties present their claims and arguments.
- The mediator/arbitrator helps both sides communicate effectively.
- If an agreement is reached, it is documented and legally recognized.

Step 4: Implementing the Resolution

- In mediation, parties voluntarily implement the settlement.
- In arbitration and Lok Adalats, the decision is **legally binding**.

9.5 How to Find ADR Services in India

- **Mediation Centres:** Most high courts have mediation centres that handle property disputes.
- **Legal Services Authorities:** National Legal Services Authority (NALSA) and state-level legal bodies organize Lok Adalats.
- **Private Arbitration Firms:** Many law firms offer arbitration services for faster resolutions.
- **Online Dispute Resolution Platforms:** Websites like **Presolv360, Centre for Online Dispute Resolution (CODR), and Sama** provide online mediation and arbitration services.

9.6 Conclusion

ADR methods such as mediation and arbitration provide faster, more cost-effective solutions to property disputes compared to traditional litigation. By reducing the burden on courts and fostering amicable resolutions, ADR can be a valuable tool for families looking to settle conflicts while preserving relationships. However, awareness and accessibility of ADR options remain limited. As we conclude this book in the final chapter, we will reflect on the key insights gained and discuss practical steps individuals and families can take to prevent property disputes and manage them effectively.

Key Takeaways — Chapter 9

ADR methods — mediation, arbitration, and Lok Adalats — can resolve property disputes far more quickly and at far lower cost than court litigation. ADR is especially appropriate when both parties are willing to negotiate, when preserving family relationships matters, and when the issue involves asset division rather than criminal fraud. Online dispute resolution platforms such as Presolv360 and Sama now allow parties in different cities or countries to resolve disputes digitally. NALSA organises Lok Adalats across India that provide accessible and often cost-free resolution for many property cases. Choosing ADR over litigation is not a concession — it is frequently the most practical and humane path to resolution.

Chapter 10: Conclusion

In this book, we have examined the multifaceted phenomenon of property disputes in Indian families. We have traced their historical roots, explored the psychology behind them, and navigated the intricate legal landscape that governs them.

Property disputes within Indian families are not just legal battles; they are deeply personal conflicts that have shaped history, strained relationships, and consumed generations in prolonged litigation. As we have seen throughout this book, these disputes arise from a combination of historical legacies, psychological factors, legal complexities, and the evolving socio-economic landscape of India.

From the epic tales of the Ramayana and Mahabharata to modern corporate feuds, family property battles have been a recurring theme in Indian society. Psychological underpinnings such as sibling rivalries, parental favouritism, and unresolved childhood grievances often serve as the foundation for these disputes. The legal system, while offering structured mechanisms for resolution, remains overburdened with millions of pending cases, making property disputes one of the longest-drawn legal battles in the country.

The complexities of property laws, including succession, transfer, and litigation procedures, highlight the necessity of clear legal planning. While the Indian legal framework provides avenues for inheritance and ownership transfer through wills, partition, and alternative dispute resolution mechanisms, many families still find themselves entangled in bitter court battles due to ambiguities, emotional conflicts, and fraudulent dealings.

However, there are ways to prevent these disputes and protect family relationships. Some of the ways mentioned in the book are summarized below:

- **Plan Early and Clearly**: A legally sound will is the most effective way to prevent inheritance disputes. Clearly documenting property ownership and succession plans can reduce misunderstandings and ensure smooth transitions.

- **Understand Your Legal Rights**: Awareness of property rights, especially for women and NRIs, is crucial. Educating oneself about inheritance laws, co-ownership rules, and land registration processes can prevent exploitation and legal complications.

- **Use Mediation and Alternative Dispute Resolution (ADR)**: Courts are not always the best place to resolve family disputes. Mediation and ADR mechanisms can provide quicker, less expensive, and more amicable solutions.

- **Protect Your Property from Encroachment and Fraud**: Property fraud, illegal occupations, and unauthorized transfers are rampant, particularly in cases involving absentee owners. Regular legal checks, proper documentation, and legal safeguards can help prevent such situations.

- **Emphasize Family Communication**: Open discussions about inheritance and property distribution among family members can prevent bitterness and legal battles. Transparency and fairness in decision-making can reduce future conflicts.

- **Seek Legal Advice When Needed**: Engaging a competent lawyer early in a dispute can prevent costly legal mistakes and unnecessary delays. Professional legal guidance ensures that one's rights are protected within the framework of the law.

Ultimately, property is a material asset, but relationships are invaluable. No legal victory can truly compensate for the loss of trust and family bonds that prolonged disputes create. While legal frameworks and judicial interventions are necessary, the true resolution of property conflicts lies in a blend of legal prudence, psychological understanding, and open dialogue within families. By fostering a culture of legal awareness, financial planning, and mutual respect, Indian families can ensure that property remains a source of security rather than a cause for strife.

To conclude, we hope this book has provided valuable insights into the historical, psychological, and legal aspects of property disputes in India. More importantly, we hope it inspires individuals and families to take proactive steps in safeguarding their assets while preserving family harmony. Property battles may be inevitable, but with the right approach, they don't have to be destructive. The future of family wealth and relationships depends on how we navigate these challenges today.

Glossary of Key Legal Terms

The following is a brief reference guide to key legal terms used throughout this book.

Intestate: Dying without leaving a valid will. When a person dies intestate, the law of succession determines how their property is distributed among their heirs.

Testator: A person who has made and executed a legally valid will.

Probate: The legal process by which a deceased person's will is verified by a court as authentic, and the executor is granted authority to distribute the estate as directed in the will.

Executor: A person named in a will who is responsible for carrying out the instructions of the testator and administering the estate after death.

Adverse Possession: A legal doctrine under which a person who occupies another's land openly and continuously for a specified period (12 years in India) may acquire legal title to that land.

Power of Attorney (PoA): A legal document authorising one person (the agent) to act on behalf of another (the principal) in legal or financial matters. A General PoA grants broad powers; a Specific or Limited PoA restricts the agent to named transactions.

Mediation: A voluntary, confidential dispute resolution process in which a neutral third party (the mediator) helps the parties in a dispute reach a mutually acceptable settlement. Unlike arbitration, the mediator does not impose a decision.

Arbitration: A private, binding dispute resolution process in which one or more arbitrators hear evidence and arguments from both parties and issue a legally enforceable decision (an "award").

Lok Adalat: Literally "People's Court," a statutory alternative dispute resolution forum in India organised under the Legal Services Authorities Act 1987. Awards passed by Lok Adalats are final, binding, and cannot be appealed in any court. They are free of cost to the parties.

Encroachment: The unlawful intrusion upon, or occupation of, another person's land or property, either partially (such as by constructing a wall or structure that crosses a boundary) or wholly (by taking possession of the property).

Wakalatnama: A formal document filed in court authorising a specific advocate to appear and argue on behalf of a party in legal proceedings.

Ancestral Property: Property inherited from one's parents, grandparents, or great-grandparents without division across four generations. Under the Hindu Succession Act, coparceners (members of a joint Hindu family) have a birthright share in ancestral property.

RERA (Real Estate Regulatory Authority): Established under the Real Estate (Regulation and Development) Act 2016, RERA is a statutory body that regulates the real estate sector in India, protects buyers from builder fraud, and provides a fast-track grievance redressal mechanism.

About the Authors

Siva Prasad Bose is an author of various introductory guidebooks related to aspects of Indian laws. He is currently retired after many years of service in Uttar Pradesh Power Corporation Limited. He received his engineering degree from Jadavpur University, Kolkata and has a law degree from Meerut University, Meerut. His interests lie in the fields of family law, civil law, law of contracts, and areas of law related to power grid and electricity revenue related issues.

Joy Bose is a researcher and data scientist by profession, with expertise in machine learning and a masters degree in law from Golden Gate University. He has co-authored this book drawing on his interest in the social and legal dimensions of family disputes in India.

Other Books by Siva Prasad Bose

Introduction to Wills and Probate

Senior Citizens Abuse in India

Introduction to negotiable instruments

Introduction to marriage laws in India

Neighbor Problems in India and what to do about them

Managing Court Cases with Mental Strength

Delays in Court Cases in India

Introduction to Patents and Patent Law in India

www.ingramcontent.com/pod-product-compliance
Lightning Source LLC
Chambersburg PA
CBHW070117230526
45472CB00004B/1297